CAN YOU HEAR
THE TREES TALKING?

CAN YOU HEAR THE TREES TALKING?

DISCOVERING THE HIDDEN LIFE OF THE FOREST

PETER WOHLLEBEN

Translated by **SHELLEY TANAKA**

GREYSTONE KIDS

GREYSTONE BOOKS • VANCOUVER/BERKELEY/LONDON

CONTENTS

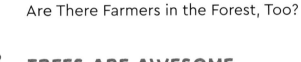

LET'S GO ON A
JOURNEY OF DISCOVERY

I'VE BEEN LEADING GROUPS OF CHILDREN through the forest for the past twenty-six years. And I always find it boring to simply explain the differences between the trees. Isn't it much more exciting to bite into them and taste the difference? Or how about exploring the forest internet? There really is such a thing, and the trees use it to exchange news. Not only that, but they live in families, help each other out, and can even count. That sounds like a fairy tale, but it's true. The forest is exciting, and so much more than just some old trees. I show this to children in my forest school, and now I'm showing you in this book.

As we take our stroll through the forest, we'll also pay attention to the animals living there. Which animals live way up high and which hide in leaves? Which have phenomenal memories and which farm other animals?

Because it's always good to figure things out for yourself, and because solving puzzles is fun, there are lots of activities to try and fascinating quizzes to answer. We'll also take trips to faraway places around the world—and into cities close to home. You can be a researcher there as well as out in the forest.

I really enjoyed writing this book. I particularly enjoyed the day when Elias, Jonathan, Nele, Mia, Finn, Miko, Romy, Sophie, Jan, and I went out into the forest together to experiment with some of the activities I've described in these pages. We laughed a lot as we tried many of them out. And I realized

that even after you've read this book and done all the activities, the forest is still an amazing place to be. After we blew through a log and soap bubbles came out (yes, it worked!), Romy suddenly found wood really exciting, and she began to collect samples from different tree species to take home with her.

There's something new to see in the forest every day—even for me as a forester. Come along with me as we explore together. Let's set off on our adventure!

— Peter Wohlleben

> In this book, I'll show you how to explore and investigate things in the forest. But when you do this, you should always take an adult with you. And you should never put anything from the forest in your mouth unless an adult can identify what it is, as some plants can be poisonous. If you have food allergies, it's best to avoid forest snacks altogether.

Chapter 1

HOW TREES WORK

A TREE HAS A HUGE BODY. And, just like yours, that body is made up of many different parts. It has structures that are similar to your skeleton, blood vessels, and skin. But what does it do, say, when it wants to take a breath of air? Or a drink of water? And how do trees grow to be so big, anyway?

HOW DO TREES BREATHE?

Leaves are very important to trees, because trees use their leaves to make their food. When trees are hungry—and they're always hungry—they just hold their leaves up to the light.

LEAVES MIX WATER WITH CERTAIN PARTS of the air to make sugar. To do that, they need energy, and they get this energy from light.

Wait a minute. Leaves use air? Does this mean they can breathe just like you? Yes, leaves breathe in and out—through their mouths, which they can open and shut. These mouths even have lips, just like yours. But there is one big difference. A tree doesn't have just one mouth—it has thousands. They're all very tiny, and they're located on the undersides of the leaves. When it's very hot and dry, trees close their mouths because they lose lots of water when they breathe, just like you do. (You can see this if you breathe on a windowpane—the moisture from your breath will fog the glass.)

This is what tree mouths look like under a microscope.

*

Larches are one of just three conifers that turn yellow in the fall and shed their needles for the winter.

If you close your mouth, you won't suffocate, because you can still breathe through your nose. When it's dry outside and a tree shuts its many mouths, it doesn't suffocate either, because it can still take in air through its bark and roots.

The upper surface of the leaves has a waxy coating, which often makes them shiny. The sun shines on the tops of the leaves, and because the leaves are so thin, they can easily dry out. The wax makes them thicker so they can hold in moisture, and this keeps them healthy.

The leaves of each species of tree look different. Hornbeam leaves, for example, have notched edges like a saw. Others—such as oak leaves—have wavy edges.

There's also a big difference between deciduous trees and conifers. Deciduous trees have big, flat leaves. The leaves of conifers are narrow and pointed, like needles—and they can prick you. This is how conifers protect themselves so that deer won't eat them.

In the winter, deciduous trees drop their leaves, but conifers hold onto their needles. They do this because many of them live where it's very cold. The winters are long and the summers are very short. So it's better for the trees to stay green the whole time. That way they can start to make sugar whenever a warm day arrives. If they had to wait to grow new leaves first, summer would be over before they had time to make any food.

Flat leaves are very sensitive, and they really don't like cold weather. The leaves of deciduous trees such as oak and beech would freeze on the first frosty day. That's why these trees drop their leaves before winter. The needles of spruce trees and other conifers contain oil that protects them from freezing.

*

But there are a few conifers that behave like deciduous trees: the larch, the dawn redwood, and the bald cypress. In the fall, their needles turn yellow and fall off. That's why a lot of people think these trees are dead when they see them in winter. Really, they're just sleeping through the cold time of year.

Look!

Leaves Large and Small

TREES LIVE IN MANY DIFFERENT environments—dry or wet, hot or cold—and the shape and size of their leaves is important. In tropical rain forests, large leaves with pointed tips shed water easily when it rains. In desert regions, feathery leaflets with a small surface area lose moisture slowly in the hot sun.

Quiz

Which tree has more leaves or needles?
* **Spruce**
* **Beech**

Spruce. A beech tree has only about 200,000 leaves, but a full-grown spruce can have more than 10 million needles. That's because spruce needles are much smaller than beech leaves. To catch the same amount of sunlight as a beech tree, a spruce needs to have many more needles than the beech tree has leaves.

HOW DO TREES DRINK?

Just like other living things, trees need water. And because they are the elephants of the plant world, they need a lot of it. On a hot summer day, a large beech tree can easily drink up three or four bathtubs full of water.

OF COURSE, THERE ARE NO BATHTUBS in the forest, which means that beech trees have to get every drop of water from the ground. They do this using their roots to feel for the spots where it's nice and moist.

Once they've found a moist spot, they quickly suck up all the water. And to make sure they really do get every last drop, the roots team up with fungi. Fungi grow fine threads around the roots of these forest giants and, like cotton balls, they soak up even more water for the trees. Different salts from the ground are carried into the tree trunks along with the water. The trees need these salts to grow, and they like them. It's like when you eat chips—once you start, you can't stop!

We still don't really know how trees get water all the way up to their crowns. (Maybe you'll want to research this yourself when you get older.) What scientists do know is that it takes a lot of energy for trees to do this—more energy than you would need to blow up a balloon as big as a house.

*

In the winter, when the water in the ground freezes, the trees take a break from drinking. After all, you can't drink ice cubes. That's why, before they grow leaves again in the spring, they suck a whole lot of water up into their trunks in one big gulp. If you take a stethoscope (that thing the doctor uses to listen to your heart) and hold it up against the bark, you may

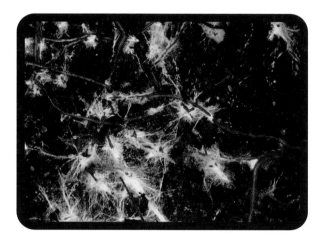

actually be able to hear the water rushing up inside the tree. As soon as the tree leafs out, the water pressure drops back down.

*

Trees that belong to the same species usually drink about the same amount. But some learn to drink a little less. During a hot summer, the ground can dry out. If a tree keeps trying to suck water from dry soil, its wood may crack. That helps it learn to do a better job of managing its water supply. Come the next spring, instead of drinking up all the water in May and June, it saves some for July and August.

Some trees learn more quickly than others. There are reckless trees that drink a lot, and careful trees that prefer to conserve water. Fortunately, the careful trees are very nice to the others. When they notice that the ground is drying out, they warn their fellow trees through the fungi that act as the forest internet. (You can read all about this in Chapter 3.) When the news gets out, even trees that like to guzzle water begin to cut back.

*

The forest's water supply is constantly refilled by rain and snow. To catch every possible drop of rain, deciduous trees such as beech and oak angle their branches up into the air to act as big funnels. The rain runs along their branches to the trunk, where it shoots down to the ground. Sometimes so much water runs down the trunk that it froths up when it hits the ground.

Conifers are not as good at catching rain. Many of them come from colder places, so they're better prepared for snow than for dry weather. After a snowfall, their flexible branches hang down close to their trunks so the tree doesn't fall over under the heavy snow.

This doesn't work with deciduous trees. Their branches reach up to the sky, and they would break off under a heavy load of snow. That's why these trees drop their leaves in the fall. Then the snow can simply fall between the bare branches right onto the ground.

The branches of conifers work well to shed snow, but not so well to catch rain. Because conifers are narrow at the top and their branches angle out or down rather than up, they act like umbrellas. This means the ground around the trunks of conifers often stays very dry, and in the summer the trees can be very thirsty.

Look!

Being Thirsty Hurts!

A thirsty tree's trunk can tear when it tries to suck water from dry ground.

IF IT'S A VERY DRY SUMMER and spruces continue to suck water out of the ground, especially greedy trees can split open along the length of their trunks. That's a bad injury for a tree. Thick drops of pitch seep out of the wound (pitch is like the blood of the spruce tree), and the wound never really heals. That tree will have a long, seeping scar down its bark for the rest of its life.

With their wide crowns, beech trees can capture a lot of rain and direct it down their trunks to the ground.

CAN TREES GET THINNER?

A full-grown tree is very heavy. It can weigh more than five cars, and its trunk needs to be really strong so it doesn't collapse under all that weight.

Big trees like this southern live oak need wide trunks to support the weight of their crowns.

THAT'S WHY A TREE IS MADE of wood inside. Wood for a tree is a bit like your bones are for you. You could say that its wood is its skeleton. If you didn't have any bones, you'd be floppy like a rag doll, and you wouldn't be able to stand up. The same goes for the tree: it needs its wood to stand up straight. And because wood is so strong, it can support a tree even when it grows really tall.

*

If you take a look at a tree that's been cut down, you'll see that its trunk is made up of a series of rings. Each year a new circle of wood grows under the tree's bark, and the trunk grows wider and wider.

You can tell from these rings how old the tree was when it was cut down. Count the rings from the outside to the middle—the middle ring is the tree when it was one year old.

Of course, you can't count the rings when a tree is still alive because they're under the bark—you can only see them after the tree has been cut down.

*

Once wood is there, it doesn't go away. Because a trunk only grows around the outside, in a thin layer between the bark and the wood, everything already inside the trunk stays the same. And so a tree never gets thinner, only thicker.

That's a good thing, because the tree is also growing taller, and that means it's getting heavier. It needs a sturdy trunk to support its weight, just like you need a strong skeleton to support your growing body. That's why adults are stronger than children, and older trees are stronger than younger ones.

*

There's something else trees have that makes them similar to people. Your blood flows through tiny tubes called arteries that run from your heart to every part

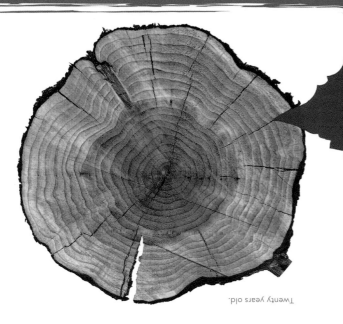

Twenty years old.

Quiz

How old is this tree? Count the rings from the outside to the middle.

* Ten years old
* Twenty years old
* Thirty years old

of your body. Trees have to pump water from their roots all the way up to their crowns, so they have an extensive system of tiny tubes, too, called vessels. You might be able to see these water vessels if you look at the rings in a piece of wood—they look like small holes.

But water only flows in the tree's outermost rings. That's why in the summer, if everything is working properly, a tree will be quite wet under its bark. Farther inside, the wood becomes drier. Nothing's happening there anymore, and the tree can't feel anything there, either. That's why it doesn't really matter if the inner wood begins to rot. Even if its trunk becomes hollowed out like an empty pipe, the tree will still be just fine.

*

But there's one more question. Why does a tree need a trunk at all? Couldn't its crown grow straight out of its roots?

A tree needs a trunk so it can grow taller than all the other plants around it. Otherwise it would just be a bush. (Bushes don't have trunks.) Since they're the tallest plants in the world, trees don't need to be afraid of other plants. They can grow above them all—except for other trees, of course. (We'll find out later why there are some anxious oaks out there.)

TRY THIS! ⬆

FIND A BIRCH LOG. If your family buys firewood, it will often have birch logs in it—you can recognize them by their white and black bark. If you don't have any firewood at home, ask your friends who have fireplaces or fire pits.

Spread some dish detergent over one end of the log. Now press your lips against the other end and blow. If the experiment works properly, you'll see soap bubbles coming out. That happens because the air you blow travels through the water vessels in the wood until it reaches the soapy film at the other end.

WHY DON'T TREES FALL OVER?

A tree is a trunk with branches and twigs on it. Leaves or needles grow on the twigs. But something really important is missing from this description: the roots. They're the first part of a tree to grow.

AS SOON AS A SEED SPROUTS, a small root tip grows down into the ground. It feels its way around to find the best place to keep growing. (Roots like soft, loose, damp soil the best.) The root spreads out and divides.

As the root divides, it grows fine hairs along its length that increase its surface area so it can suck up more water from the soil. These hairs dry out very easily—that's why if you bring a baby tree home from the nursery to plant in your yard, you have to be very careful not to expose the roots to air for more than five to ten minutes. If the roots are bare and not covered in soil, the best thing is to wrap a plastic bag around them until the hole for the tree is dug and you're ready to plant it. A tree needs healthy roots if it is to grow tall and strong.

Those cottony fungal threads I mentioned earlier don't just grow around the root tips—they grow right into the roots. This doesn't hurt the tree, though. In fact, it's nice for the tree because it knows the fungi are helping it. Not only do the fungi help the tree suck up water, they also guide the roots through the ground and show them the best places to grow.

*

As a tree gets older, its trunk gets wider. Its roots do, too, and they become as stiff and hard as branches. They need to be, because now they must support the weight of a heavy trunk and a large crown.

As long as there's no wind, that's not too difficult. On a calm day, the tree stands tall on its roots the way

You can see the fine roots on this toppled tree. They help the tree find water underground.

you stand on your own two feet. It's easy as long as the trunk is growing nice and straight.

Some trees, though, are quite crooked. And because they're so heavy, they can easily topple over. That's why the roots of a crooked tree quickly grow thicker near the trunk so they can support it. It's like when you spread your feet apart a bit to get better balance. That's what the tree does, too.

Whenever a storm blows, the wind tears hard at any tree in its way. Imagine the force of fifty cars trying to push the tree over. It can only survive if it has strong roots, which hold the tree down like thick ropes holding down a big tent. Except roots can withstand much more pressure.

If you find a tree that has fallen over in the forest, take a look at its roots. If the tree is a spruce or a Douglas fir, the roots will often be spread out in the shape of a large, flat plate. No wonder the tree fell over—to provide firm support, roots must grow deep down into the ground.

Sometimes a tree stump will show you just how important the roots are. In fact, they're the most important part of the tree. Why? Because often a shoot will grow out of an old stump, and this shoot can grow up to be an adult tree. It's really the same tree, except now it has a whole new trunk.

*

Roots may be very strong, but they're also sensitive. They really don't like it when people walk on them or, even worse, when cars drive over them. They may get squashed and even injured. Diseases could get into their wounds and spread through their trunks. Then the tree will die before it has a chance to grow old.

Look!
Strong Roots

SOME TREE ROOTS ARE GIGANTIC. The roots of the Moreton Bay fig are so enormous you could easily play hide-and-seek in them. These enormous roots support enormous crowns: the branches can spread out a hundred feet (30 m) or more. Roots can extend far below the surface, as well. In its search for life-giving water, a wild fig in the Echo Caves in South Africa has grown roots a record four hundred feet (122 m) deep— deeper than a football field is long.

Quiz

Can trees grow if their roots are always underwater?

* **No. How would they breathe?**

* **Yes. Trees are really clever at adapting to different environments.**

Yes. The bald cypress can grow in swampy places thanks to "snorkels" on their roots that let them breathe even when they're submerged, just like you would use a snorkel if you wanted to breathe underwater.

 Chapter 2

GROWING UP IN THE FOREST

MANY ANIMALS LIVE IN FAMILIES,
just like you. But what about trees?
How do mother trees know where
their children are? How do trees share
food with their aunts, uncles, and
grandparents? And what are their
secrets for living to a grand old age?

HOW DO TREES MAKE BABIES?

Most trees like to live in families, and in each family there are—of course—children!
That's why trees work to grow strong—so they can have babies. You can see this
for yourself when they're in bloom.

Pine trees release so much pollen,
it can look like a cloud of dust.

IN THE SPRING IT CAN BE dusty under trees, and you may find your shoes covered with a layer of tiny, yellowy-green particles. That's male pollen— tiny grains that want to land on female blossoms. Pollen grains are carried by the wind, so they can't really seek out blossoms themselves. When they meet a female blossom, it's by accident. That's why a tree must produce a huge amount of pollen, so that a few grains will reach their goal.

With most trees, the female blossoms are on the same tree that produces the male pollen. They share the same "house," so to speak. With some trees, such as the willow, trees are either male or female—the male trees produce pollen and don't grow blossoms, and the female trees grow blossoms and don't produce pollen— but this is the exception.

*

After the female blossoms are successfully pollinated, seeds develop. By fall the seeds of beech and oak trees are mature, and they drop to the ground, where many hungry animals are waiting for these delicious treats. Wild boars in particular adore beechnuts and acorns because they're full of fat and oil that help them build up a thick layer of fat of their own. This way the animals carry their winter food supply under their skin, and they can go for a few days without finding anything to eat.

*

Tree parents aren't too happy about all this because, after all, their children are supposed to grow from these seeds. That's why some trees, such as beeches, decide among themselves when they will bloom.

Some years their branches have no seeds, and many wild boars don't survive the winter. But every three to five years, all the beech trees bloom like crazy at the same time. There are lots of beechnuts—so many that the wild boars can't eat them all.

We don't know how trees communicate with each other over hundreds of miles to coordinate when they will and will not bloom. (You're going to be seeing more of these we-just-don't-knows in the course of this book, because we still have so much to learn about what goes on in the forest.)

*

With beeches and oaks, the seeds fall straight down from the mother tree. That way the tree family stays together nicely. But some tree species are loners. Willows, poplars, and birches like to stand on their own. To make sure their children can grow up far away, they produce seeds that are very tiny and covered with small hairs or fluff, so they can be easily caught up in a gust of wind and carried several miles away.

Other seeds, such as those of maples or many conifers, are too big and heavy to simply blow away. So these trees have come up with another strategy: each seed is equipped with wings. That way the seed can spin like a helicopter propeller in the air. Even without a motor, the seed can slowly float to the ground, and if it's caught up in a strong wind, it can fly a few hundred yards.

Look!

Tree Seeds

LARGE SEEDS WITHOUT WINGS OR FUZZ prefer to fall beneath their mother tree. Beechnuts, for example, like to stay close to home. Smaller seeds with propellers, like the maple seeds pictured here, or tiny, fluffy seeds like those of the willow, fly far away from the mother tree. The children of these trees don't mind growing up without family close by.

Quiz

What is the greatest number of seeds that a quaking aspen tree can produce each year?

* **Five thousand**
* **26 million**

26 million. The seeds are very tiny, so the tree can produce a lot of them. And the more seeds that are sent out to drift on the wind, the greater the chance they'll find a good place to grow.

DO TREES HAVE GRANDPARENTS?

If you come from a big family, you probably have lots of other relatives besides your parents. You might have siblings, cousins, aunts and uncles, and grandparents, too. But how do the trees in the forest know who is related to whom?

WHEN IT COMES TO TREES, THAT'S much harder to figure out than it is for humans. After all, we can ask questions and get answers. And sometimes family members look so much alike that we know even without asking that people are related.

Trees recognize each other differently. They communicate with each other through their roots below the ground. Trees can feel more through the tips of their roots than we can with our fingers. They can even make decisions with them! A root tip is almost like a small brain.

If a tree's roots meet those of a neighboring tree, they can check whether they belong to the same species. If so, then those trees are probably part of the same family. Now their roots will grow together. The trees can send messages and exchange the sugar they have made through this connection. It's as if they had invited each other to dinner.

*

It's nice to have family and friends, but not all trees like each other. Some prefer not to share.

You can look at old tree stumps to see which trees belong to a community and which stand alone. If the bark is falling off and the stump is rotten, the tree is out of touch with its neighbors. If the edge of an old stump is very hard and still has solid bark, the stump is still alive. That's only possible when the stump is getting food from its family through its roots.

This is what true tree friends look like. They stand close together and help each other.

Some stumps can stay alive for hundreds of years like this. They may be the grandparents of the younger trees around them.

*

It's likely that old trees and stumps can remember things that happened long ago. They've experienced a lot that they can pass on to their younger family members. They may have learned, for instance, how to share the water in the soil during a dry summer so that no trees will die of thirst.

Sometimes two related trees like each other so much that they can no longer live separately. They grow with their roots so tightly interwoven that they become like a single tree. Their crowns face away from each other so they don't get in each other's way.

With conifers, pairs that seem to be closely linked might not actually be. Conifers grow thinner branches in the direction of their neighbors, which makes it look as though they're being considerate of each other, even though they may not be friends underground.

*

Tree families only work this way if we don't disturb them. When trees are cut down, the ones that are left lose their relatives.

Imagine three trees standing in a row. They're all connected underground and can talk to each other through their roots. If the middle tree is cut down, that connection is broken. And even though the two remaining trees are not that far apart, they can no longer send messages—or sugar—to each other through their roots.

That's why it's always best to leave old trees alone.

TRY THIS!

WITH DECIDUOUS TREES YOU CAN RECOGNIZE real partners by their branches. Two trees standing side by side will turn their thick crown branches away from each other. This happens rarely, though, so you may have to search for a while. If you find a pair of trees like this, take a photo or sketch the two crowns. For comparison, you can draw or photograph two trees that are not friendly. And because true tree partners are so rare, you can share pictures with your friends to see who has spotted the most.

Look!

Old Tree Stump

HOW CAN YOU RECOGNIZE AN OLD tree stump? A fresh stump has hard wood in the middle, and often it is still light-colored. With an old stump, the wood is already dark and rotten, and it breaks up easily when you touch it. If an old stump is still alive, the bark around the outside edge will be tightly attached. If the bark on the outside is falling off, it means the tree is dead.

These two trees are growing together, connected by their roots.

WHAT DO TREE CHILDREN LEARN AT SCHOOL?

Tree children go to school together in the shade of their mothers, where they learn how to grow very old. School lasts much longer for them than it does for you. It isn't over for two hundred to three hundred years!

TREE CHILDREN ARE NEVER ALONE in an old-growth forest (one in which a tree has never been cut down). Here all the trees and animals can live as they wish.

When small trees sprout from seeds in this kind of forest, many do so at the same time, creating a tree nursery. Their mothers stand over them, seeking out their children with their roots underground.

Once they find the roots of their children, they connect with them. Then the tree children are nursed by their mothers. But instead of receiving breast milk like human children, they receive sugar water. They need this because in an old-growth forest, it's very

dark at ground level. With so little light, the tree children can't produce their own sugar with their leaves, so they have to rely on their parents.

*

The large crowns of mother trees make it dark on the forest floor. In the dark, young trees can only grow very slowly. Slow-growing trees do not wear themselves out as quickly as faster-growing ones, leaving them with enough energy to live to be five hundred years old or even older. (You can find out more about the oldest known living tree in Chapter 4.)

School starts for tree children when they're about three feet (1 m) tall. Their most important subject isn't language arts or math, but "growing straight." That might sound funny, but a tree has to grow straight so that it won't break during a heavy storm later on. If the trunk is crooked, then the wood inside becomes very cramped. It might feel to the tree the way a sore muscle does to you. If a storm bends a tree like this, its trunk can break at those tight spots.

That's why mother trees want their children to grow straight up.

Here's how it works. About a hundred tree students stand close together. They have to stretch right up if they're going to catch at least a little sunlight from above.

But every class has its class clown. They don't listen to the old trees, and sometimes they grow to the left, sometimes to the right. Who knows whether the other trees find this funny, but that's not important. What is important is that the other trees carry on slowly growing, up past their crooked classmates.

Eventually things grow even darker for the class clowns—too dark. No tree can live without light. That's why the crooked trees will die at some point. After three hundred years, of the hundred students, only one or two will be left, just waiting for old trees to die and make way for them. Then these model students can become very tall and very old themselves.

*

In most forests today, tree classrooms no longer work properly because many mother trees are cut down. That means tree children can grow up crooked and, what's even worse, they grow very quickly, because they get a lot of light. Lots of light means they can make a lot of sugar.

Maybe all this sweetness makes them happy. But after two hundred or three hundred years (and for a tree that isn't really a long time), these trees will die because they've lived such unhealthy lives.

TRY THIS!

If you want to know how old a small deciduous tree is, count the number of little swellings (called nodes) on one of its branches. Each node marks one year. Count along the branch from the outermost bud toward the trunk. (This works especially well with beech trees.) The branches are widest closest to the trunk, and the nodes are hardest to recognize here, so it will take a bit of guesswork. With conifers, branches grow in "floors" up the trunk, with each floor signaling another year of life.

Look!

Tree Classroom

YOU CAN SEARCH THROUGH AN OLD beech forest to find a tree classroom—a collection of small trees between three and thirty feet (1–10 m) tall. When you go into the classroom, look for students that are crooked and tilted over to one side. Some of them will have already died. You can tell by the fact that the bark is falling off their trunks. From the many small trees that once sprouted, gradually fewer and fewer will remain.

DO TREES GET PIMPLES?

Healthy wood is quite wet. Even when the hot summer sun shines on the trunk, the tree doesn't dry out because it's covered with bark, which acts like its skin.

This is what tree pimples look like. Branches once grew here. As the tree grows taller, these scars will stay at the same height because trees only grow from the top.

BARK PROTECTS A TREE JUST LIKE your skin protects you. And a tree loses water when its bark is broken, the same way you bleed when your skin is injured. That's why you should never scratch anything into a tree's bark.

The bark of each tree species looks a bit different. Beech trees have a smooth skin, while oak trees are quite rough and furrowed. But the appearance of this protective layer also depends on age—for trees just like for humans. Your skin may be smooth and wrinkle-free.

Older people like your grandparents may have many wrinkles. Laugh lines may form around their eyes, because people pull up their cheeks and crinkle the skin under their eyes when they laugh.

I don't know whether or not trees laugh. But they do get wrinkles as they age. Once beech trees are more than two hundred years old, their smooth trunks become cracked and ridged. This happens much earlier for oak trees. They can get deep wrinkles when they're just twenty years old!

Such wrinkles occur because trees get a little wider every year. If their bark didn't grow as they put on more layers of wood, it would rip open like a shirt that's too small. To make sure this doesn't happen, the bark grows at the same rate as the tree does when it puts on its new growth ring each year. But because the old bark on the outside is dead, it can't expand as the tree grows new wood and bark underneath it, so it splits apart, forming wrinkles.

*

All skin flakes off, including yours. Thousands of small pieces of skin fall from your arms, legs, head, and stomach every day, because you're always growing new skin. It's the same with trees. Some species, such as beech and spruce, lose an especially large amount of bark—their trunks always look quite smooth because only the fresh bark is left. With oak and pine trees, much less old bark flakes off. A thick layer of old bark stays on the trunk, and when it gets too tight, it bursts open and creates deep furrows. So wrinkles not only reflect a tree's age, but also its species.

Over a tree's lifetime, scarring forms on the bark. These scars can tell you what the tree has experienced. The most common types of scar are the ones left where a branch used to be. A dead branch will eventually fall off, and the tree closes the hole in the trunk with new wood and new bark. Then an oval scar forms on the bark, which looks like a pimple on the trunk. You can tell how big the branch was from the size of the scar: the length of the scar from top to bottom will be twice the diameter of the branch that fell off.

TRY THIS!

YOU CAN MAKE A SCRAPBOOK of bark from different tree species. Press a piece of paper against the bark with one hand. With your other hand, rub a crayon over the paper to make a colorful impression of the bark on the page. You can make and collect different bark pictures this way.

Look!

Peels and Curls

MOST TREES HAVE FLAKY SKIN, but some have skin that peels off instead. The rust-brown bark of arbutus (also called madrone) trees, which grow in the Pacific Northwest, curls away to reveal bright-green new bark underneath that's silky smooth to the touch. The silvery bark of paper birch peels off in layers that look like very thin sheets of paper.

Chapter 3

FRIENDS AND ENEMIES IN THE FOREST

THERE ARE FIERCE STRUGGLES GOING on in the forest every day, and trees are busy sending out news bulletins to keep their friends up to date. In summer, if you're lucky, you might even be able to smell some of the messages they exchange. Others you'll never pick up on because they're passed along underground.

CAN TREES TALK?

Sometimes things get dangerous in the forest. For example, if small beetles arrive, they can eat holes in a tree's bark and kill the tree. Fortunately, however, trees close ranks and help each other out.

This tree is just noticing that a giraffe is eating its leaves. Because it will take a few minutes for its poison to reach the leaves, the giraffe can still snack for a while.

IT'S EASIEST TO DEFEND YOURSELF when you know that someone is coming. And that's exactly why trees talk to each other.

A single tree notices when something bites it. After the initial shock, the tree will taste who is nibbling on it. Yes, you read that right: trees can taste. Because whenever an animal bites into the bark, a leaf, or a branch, it injects a bit of saliva into the wound. And every animal's spit tastes different.

It may sound disgusting, but the tree knows what to do when this happens. Right away it begins to pump liquid into the bite site—liquid that tastes bad or is even poisonous. Bark beetles nibbling on the tree will often stop eating and disappear.

Trees attacked by bark beetles also release a sticky, bitter substance called pitch that beetles get stuck in. So that other trees can be on their guard, the attacked tree will call out, "Beetle alert!" Because it has no mouth to talk, the tree does this through the language of scent. The scent reaches the surrounding trees, so they can start producing pitch even before the beetles arrive.

*

In Africa, trees even defend themselves against giraffes. Giraffes love to feast on the leaves from the crowns of umbrella thorn acacias—big trees that look like umbrellas. Within just a few minutes, the trees notice something is eating them and pump poison into their leaves. That poison could kill the giraffes, so they'll quickly move on to neighboring trees.

But what if these trees know the giraffes are on the way? While the trees that are being eaten are pumping poison into their leaves, they're also giving off a gas to warn their neighbors that there are hungry giraffes about. Then the neighboring trees pump poison into their leaves, too. The giraffes know the trees will be communicating with each other, and so they'll keep walking until they're at least a hundred yards away, out of reach of the scent message, to where the leaves are still delicious. If a wind is blowing, the giraffes will seek neighboring trees that are upwind, because they know that those trees will not have received the scent message carried on the breeze.

*

Some trees, such as the elm, will even call on animals for help. If caterpillars start to nibble on its leaves, an elm can tell which kind they are. So the tree calls on the enemies of these caterpillars: small wasps that lay their eggs inside the caterpillars. The eggs hatch larvae, which eat the caterpillars from the inside out. Not a pleasant thought, maybe. Still, the elm gets rid of its enemies, and its leaves stay healthy.

Different tree species can't talk to one other. For example, beech and spruce trees are less closely related to each other than you are to goldfish. And just as you may not understand much goldfish, different tree species have little to say to each other.

TRY THIS!

FOR MANY CONIFERS, HOT SUMMER days are too warm. They become weak and more vulnerable to attacks by bark beetles. Because they aren't feeling well, they send out cries for help in scent language. You can smell these messages. The scent is spicy-sweet, like the smell that you get when you rub a few needles between your fingers.

Look!

Bite marks left by a deer

Bite Marks

ON SMALL TREES YOU CAN SOMETIMES see where buds have been removed by deer. You can tell by the fact that a small piece of bark is still hanging on the branch. Deer do not have upper incisor teeth, so they have to rip off the buds. Scientists have learned that trees can sense whether bits of their branches have been cut by a human or ripped off by a deer. A tree can taste the deer saliva and pass bitter flavors into the branch to stop the deer from nibbling. But if you cut off a branch, the tree won't waste time changing the taste of the branch. Instead, it will immediately try to repair the wound.

IS THERE A FOREST INTERNET?

Trees have no computers and no phone lines. Nevertheless, they're connected to each other, and not just through their root systems. Beneath the leaves on the forest floor, other beings have made themselves at home, and they help the trees, too.

This mushroom is the fruit of a fungus, like an apple is the fruit of an apple tree. Most of the fungus grows beneath the ground.

THESE CHATTY BEINGS ARE FUNGI. Until now it hasn't been completely clear to scientists whether fungi are more like plants or like animals. Like animals, they feed on things that were or are alive. Some fungi eat the wood of dead trees, while others prefer old leaves. But there are also species that like to partner with living trees. These fungi help trees relay messages to each other. If one tree wants to say something important to another, it sends a liquid through its roots.

Around the tips of the roots, the fungi have wrapped a soft, cottony web. This is where the fungi absorb the tree's message, and they pass it on through their fine threads. These threads run throughout the forest floor and connect the trees to each other, so that all of them can hear what the tree has to say. So,

for example, if a certain kind of beetle begins to attack one tree, other trees can get the message and prepare for it.

*

But fungi don't provide their services for nothing. Just as your internet at home has a cost, trees also have to pay for their communication system. There may not be money in the forest, but there is something similar—sugar.

Everything in the forest is crazy about sugar. Insects, birds, and fungi all love their sweets because they need sugar to grow. And trees grow their wood, leaves, and bark from sugar and from various kinds of salt. As we learned in Chapter 1, trees make this sugar using their leaves and sunlight.

*

Fungi demand up to one-third of the trees' total sugar production for their forest internet services. It's very, very expensive. But without the fungi, the trees wouldn't receive messages about imminent danger, so they pay the price. The fungi need the sugar not just because they're hungry and need to keep themselves alive, but also to produce their fleshy fruit: the mushrooms that sprout on the forest floor

every fall. If you come across a porcini, chanterelle, or bay bolete mushroom, what you're seeing is converted tree sugar.

*

So the fungal internet transports not only messages, but also sugar. If one tree wants to help another, it sends out a serving of sweets.

But the fungi don't always do what the tree wants. Sometimes they'll pass on sugar to another species of tree, and trees don't like that. They only want to help other trees of their same species.

The fungi are just playing it safe, so they don't care. It could be, for example, that one day the beech trees that they live with will all get some awful beech disease and die. Then the fungi would die, too, because they would have no more trees to supply them with sugar. So they secretly send some sugar juice to other tree species, such as oaks or birches, to make sure they stay healthy and fit. That way, if an illness breaks out among the beech trees, the fungi can offer their services to the oaks and birches, and won't need to go hungry.

Quiz

The fungal internet is spread over the whole forest floor. Fine white threads connect all the trees below the ground. If you scooped up a teaspoon of forest soil and put all the fungal threads you collected end to end, how far might they stretch?

* **One inch (2.5 cm)**
* **More than a yard (1 m)**
* **More than a mile (1.6 km)**

More than a mile. Fungal threads can be so thin that you can't see them with the naked eye.

FIND THE FUNGAL INTERNET! Push aside the upper layer of leaves on the forest floor until you can see rotted leaves, down where it's nice and humid. This is where the forest internet begins. Those thin, white strands that crisscross over each other are the cables that the trees use to send their messages. Don't worry if you pull out a few fungal threads—the forest internet won't crash. The messages will simply be diverted around the small break.

WHY DO FUNGI GROW ON TREES?

Fungi are strange things. They are neither animal nor plant, but something else. You've already met some of them that work as the forest internet. But there are also fungi that are dangerous for trees.

MANY FUNGI DON'T HELP TREES, but instead are just after their wood and sugar. For these fungi, trees are like giant pantries filled with delicious food.

But it's not so easy to get at this food, because trees can defend themselves pretty well. On the outside their bodies are covered with bark. As long as the bark isn't injured or dead, fungi can't get a foothold. Fungi like things moist, but not too moist because just like people, they need air to breathe. The water vessels running under the tree's bark keep the outer wood too wet for them. No fungi can breathe in there, and so the tree stays healthy.

*

However, often trees can be injured, such as when one falls and scrapes against the trunk of its neighbor. When this happens, the bark on the neighboring tree is scraped off, and the wood underneath dries out a bit. It takes no more than ten minutes for spores from fungi to land on the wound. These spores are like tiny seeds, and they're how fungi multiply. Spores are everywhere—even in the air you're breathing right now. They won't hurt your body, but in the

The wound in this trunk is so big that it will take many years for the tree to close it. This gives fungi a chance to invade and spread through the wood.

wound of a tree, wood-eating fungi can grow if they land on exposed wood. That's dangerous for a tree because the fungi rot its trunk. After many years, even a sturdy trunk can become as hollow as an empty pipe because the fungi have eaten all the wood inside. At some point, a hollowed-out trunk can no longer support the crown, and the tree breaks.

*

If the wound is smaller than a quarter (or, if you live in the UK, a ten-pence coin), the tree can grow new bark to cover it within two to three years. Then the wood will once again be wet enough that the fungi will die. For larger wounds, this takes much longer, and in the meantime, the fungi can spread undisturbed.

This happens very slowly, but after many years the fungi may have spread throughout the trunk and may even have penetrated through the bark to the outside. That's when you can see the fleshy fruit. They're shaped like plates and stick out of the trunk, one above the other. By the time you see these fruiting bodies on the outside of the tree, it will take only a few years before the tree will collapse.

Nevertheless, such tree fungi aren't bad for the forest, because they can't attack healthy, uninjured trees. There are also many beetles that live in the fruits of these fungi. Such beetles have become quite rare because many foresters will cut down trees as soon as they're attacked by fungi. They're afraid that the wood will be eaten, and they won't be able to sell the damaged timber later on.

*

In the city, trees attacked by fungi are cut down. Otherwise they can fall on people, houses, or cars. On roadsides, a sick tree is truly dangerous, but in the forest it's best to leave it alone. That makes those rare beetles happy! Not only that, but with fungi, things move very, very slowly. Sometimes a sick tree can get lucky and, despite having fungi, can live for another fifty years.

Quiz

How old is the oldest living fungus in the world?

* 150 years old
* 1,300 years old
* 2,400 years old

2,400 years old. It's a honey fungus that grows in the ground. Its roots have spread over an area of nearly four square miles (10 km²)—about three-quarters the size of Los Angeles International Airport—and together they weigh six hundred tons.

Tree Fungus

A TREE FUNGUS ACTS LIKE A ROOF. On the top it's waterproof. On the underside it has small holes that contain the spores. Because the spores are as fine as powder, they would clump together if they got wet, but they're well protected under the fungus roof. In dry weather they fall out and drift on the breeze to the next tree.

If a tree falls down, the fungal projections can still grow on the trunk with their roofs facing the sky to protect the holes below. Because the old sections of fungi can't move or change position, it's easy to see which have grown before and which after the tree fell to the ground.

WHAT MAKES TREES SICK?

Like humans, trees can get sick. But tree diseases are different from ours.
Beeches and oaks don't know about colds, coughs, and stomachaches.
But their illnesses can still be very stressful.

These spruces have been infested with bark beetles. Because beetles multiply so quickly and are always hungry, they kill the trees and the bark falls off.

TREES MOSTLY GET SICK THROUGH FUNGI. We've already talked about how fungi can make the trunks rotten. But there are other tiny creatures that can make trees sick as well.

If a tree is infected with bacteria, its bark often has small wounds that bleed tree blood. Tree blood looks like water. You'll only see it when the forest is dry, because in the rain the trunks are wet anyway.

If trees get sick from fungi or bacteria, they can still live for a long time if they're lucky. But you can see that they're weak. In deciduous trees, twigs and branches on the upper crown will die. That's always a sign that the tree isn't feeling well.

*

Trees often get really sick when they're attacked by animals. Sometimes beetles bore into the bark. If you can see these small holes, it's usually a sign that the tree will soon die.

It's different with conifers. Their branches don't die, but they do drop some of their needles. Healthy trees keep their needles for several years and look beautifully thick and dark green. Sick spruces and pines lose so many needles, you can see the sky through the treetops. Spruces also let their branches droop, as if they were feeling worn out.

There are a few conifers that you might think are sick or dead in the winter. Larches, dawn redwoods, and bald cypresses drop their needles the way deciduous trees lose their leaves, and look bald in the winter. But dead trees usually lose their bark, too, and that's not the case with these unusual trees. Their bark stays put.

The lines of sticky pitch running down this tree show it has successfully defended itself against a beetle attack.

And who helps the sick trees? The same way your parents look after you, other trees often look after their neighbors. The healthy ones send sugar to sick neighbors through their roots. This makes the weak trees stronger so they can fight their disease better. Helpers also live on the forest floor. Fungi fight against other fungi that grow into the tree roots and want to eat them up.

There's no real tree doctor in the forest. But it's different in the city, where people take care of sick trees. Sometimes they give them medicine or help them stand up straight by stretching ropes around the trunks and attaching them to the ground or to other trees. Sometimes the trees are given crutches —iron pipes to help support their heavy crowns.

*

Sick trees will recover if they get enough help from other trees. Some can become very old even after the whole crown has broken off. With the help of their neighbors, they can receive so much food through their roots that they'll actually slowly grow a new crown.

If a spruce defends itself successfully against bark beetles, its trunk will be covered in pitch. The beetles drown in this sticky substance as they drill into the bark. If you see intact bark with a coating of pitch on it, then you'll know that the tree won.

Look!

Moth Hunters in the Night

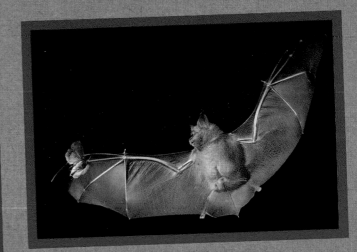

TREES ALSO HAVE ANIMAL HELPERS: for example, bats that hunt moths. Just like bats, moths fly at night, and the caterpillars of many moth species like to eat the leaves and needles of trees— sometimes so many that branches become completely bare even in the summer. This is very dangerous for the trees because without their leaves, they can no longer make food. Luckily, bats eat many insects. They can even pluck moths right off the trees.

TRY THIS!

IF YOU FIND A CONIFER WITH the bark falling off, take a piece and hold it up against the sky. You'll probably see many small holes where bark beetles have drilled their way out from the inside, after having fed under the bark when they were larvae.

Chapter 4

EVERY TREE IS DIFFERENT

IN THE FOREST IT SOMETIMES looks as though all the trees belonging to one species are the same. But, as with humans, there are timid trees and brave ones; trees that make their own way in life and trees that stand out from the crowd.

WHAT ARE TREES AFRAID OF?

The forest is full of dangers. Not for humans, so don't worry! But it's quite a different matter when it comes to trees. Insects, deer, and drought can all make life hard for them. Things become particularly difficult when different tree species fight against each other.

DOES THAT SOUND ODD, AFTER I'VE told you how well trees understand one another? How they support each other, help sick family members, and even care for old stumps? It's all true, but only when the trees belong to the same species. Beech trees help other beeches, oaks help other oaks, and so on.

But what if an oak is standing in the middle of a group of beech trees? Then it can end up in a fight—a fight, it must be said, that takes place very, very slowly. By the time it comes to an end and there is a winner and loser, many decades may have passed. If you watch the trees, you may not see much.

But wait—there is something you can see. If beech trees attack a single oak, then that tree is going to be frightened. And one tree up against several is also a bit unfair, isn't it?

*

I'll show you how to recognize fear in an oak tree. But first let's look at what the beech trees are up to. They're sending their roots beneath the roots of the oak, where they can suck away the water, leaving the oak tree quite thirsty!

The beeches are also growing their upper branches through the crown of the oak, which means the oak is unable to catch as much light with its leaves. The beeches become bigger and bigger, until one day they're taller than the oak and start casting shadows on it. You could say they're turning off the lights. Without light, the oak can't produce enough sugar

An oak tree that sprouts bushy twigs on its trunk like this is afraid. Next to it stands a beech tree, which is sucking up the water in the ground and taking light from its crown in the summer.

with its leaves. It suffers from hunger and becomes weaker and weaker, stressed, and afraid.

In its distress, the oak starts to form new branches with large leaves in clumps on its trunk. This makes

Quiz

Which trees fight against other species and are particularly hard to get along with?

* Oaks
* Beeches
* Pines

Pines. Through their roots they can send out toxins that are very unhealthy for other trees.

no sense, because down near the ground it's even darker than it is up in the crown, and so these leaves can't produce any sugar either. They start to die off. The oak is acting crazy!

This happens to people, too, when they're scared. For example, I'm afraid of big spiders, even though I know they won't hurt me.

What about you—is there anything you're afraid of? Can you understand what the oak is going through?

*

With other species it's not so easy to see when they're afraid. Sometimes two different tree species grow so close together that they wrap around each other. They look like a loving couple, but what you're seeing is actually a wrestling match—one that's carried out so slowly that we humans can't detect any movement. It's like when you look at a photo of two people embracing. You can't always tell what's going on. Are they are hugging or fighting? You can only tell if you can see them moving.

Because trees are so slow, you don't see what's really happening. Only after many decades does the loser die, and then it becomes clear that this wasn't love, but war.

That doesn't mean that trees are bad. They're just trying to do everything they can to keep themselves and their species alive.

Look!

Tree with a Temper

IF ANOTHER TREE TRIES TO GROW next to a birch tree, the birch will become annoyed. It has long, whiplike branches with small knobs on them. These knobs act like sandpaper. When the wind blows through the crown, the branches swing back and forth, beating up the crown of the neighboring tree, which loses branches and leaves and stops growing so well. Meanwhile, the birch is able to receive more light itself, and it grows even faster.

DO SOME TREES PREFER TO BE ALONE?

A single tree is not a forest. The sun shines straight onto its trunk, making it very warm. The wind quickly dries up the soil around it. Trees don't like it when this happens. And if you're alone, you get no messages from others, and no help, either.

TREES STAND ALONE FOR DIFFERENT REASONS. In the city, people plant the trees. Because we need space for our streets and homes, we plant single trees along the sidewalks. These planted trees find it difficult to talk to each other. Because there is no fungal network growing in the ground below the pavement, the forest internet doesn't work here. And because the distance between trees is usually too big, their roots don't grow together and they can't provide each other with sugar if one of them falls ill.

*

But what about in a park where there are lots of trees around? Isn't that almost the same as a forest?

If you look closely, you'll find that there are usually many different tree species in a park. But you won't find tree families. It's a bit like being at the zoo. Giraffes, lions, and elephants belong to different species. But in a zoo, the zookeepers try to keep groups of animals of the same species together. This often isn't the case in a park—there may be many trees, but only one of each species. So this kind of park is like a zoo for trees. Except unlike the animals, the trees are lonely.

These solitary trees have to grow up all by themselves, without their tree parents. That's why they grow up quickly. But trees that grow quickly as

children don't live to an old age. Even trees that might normally live for more than a thousand years in the wild will die in a park within three hundred years. That may seem like a long time, but if that tree were in an old-growth forest, its childhood would barely be over.

*

Baobabs are sometimes called upside-down trees. I think you can guess why.

Relying on Others

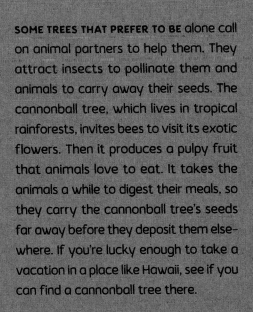

There are, however, trees that prefer to be alone. I can't imagine living a lonely life, but apple trees like it that way. If they stand very close to other apple trees, they quickly get sick. They also don't like growing in a spot where another apple tree once stood. That's why they tuck their seeds inside delicious fruits, so that animals (or you!) will take them somewhere else.

The same goes for cherry trees or mountain ashes. Birds eat the red fruits and the seeds fly away in the birds' bellies. Then when the bird deposits the seed later, along with its packet of bird-poop fertilizer, a new tree grows in that spot.

Willows, poplars, and birches let their seeds fly far away on the wind. But trees that sprout far away from their mothers grow up very quickly, as we've already seen with the city trees. That's why these loners don't grow to be very old. Their life span is 150 years at most.

SOME TREES THAT PREFER TO BE alone call on animal partners to help them. They attract insects to pollinate them and animals to carry away their seeds. The cannonball tree, which lives in tropical rainforests, invites bees to visit its exotic flowers. Then it produces a pulpy fruit that animals love to eat. It takes the animals a while to digest their meals, so they carry the cannonball tree's seeds far away before they deposit them elsewhere. If you're lucky enough to take a vacation in a place like Hawaii, see if you can find a cannonball tree there.

Quiz

Baobabs are strange-looking trees that grow where there's very little water; therefore, they need to grow far apart. What animals do baobabs in Madagascar rely on to carry their seeds away?

- Lizards
- Giant tortoises
- Bats

Giant tortoises. The tortoises eat the fruit and deposit the seeds in places where other trees aren't growing. Luckily trees are never in a hurry!

ARE SOME TREES BRAVE?

In the forest, not all trees behave the same way. Just as with humans, each tree has its own characteristics. This is particularly easy to see in the fall.

WHEN TEMPERATURES DROP IN THE AUTUMN, deciduous trees must shed their leaves, because winter can bring new dangers. If snow falls on leafy branches, they become so heavy that they can break. Sometimes the whole crown can break off, and then the tree will likely die. So the tree needs to make sure it gets rid of its leaves on time. But when is the right time, and how can trees tell when it has arrived?

Like you, trees notice that the days are getting shorter, and they feel with their skin—their bark—that the weather is getting colder. When the first frost or even snow comes, trees fall into a deep sleep.

They hibernate—the same way bears do, for example. When this happens, trees can't do anything at all. They can't even drop their leaves. So they need to check this task off their to-do list before they shut down for the winter.

*

Cautious trees discard their leaves at the beginning of October, because you never know. The first heavy snowfall might come in mid-October, so it's safer to have bare branches before then. Courageous trees wait a bit longer. There are often a few autumn days that are still warm and sunny, when they can produce more sugar with their leaves. And trees that hibernate with lots of sugar will be stronger when they wake up in the spring.

But that's also dangerous. What if it suddenly gets cold? Those brave trees will no longer be able to get rid of their leaves. You can see these unlucky trees standing around all winter with brown leaves on their branches. Every snowfall brings danger now, and I've seen many trees that have been broken because they didn't drop their leaves in time.

*

Small trees don't need to pay too much attention to this yet. They stand beneath their mothers. When it's time to go to sleep, the mother tree drops its leaves. But the tree children don't want to go to sleep yet.

Now, while the mother sleeps without foliage, lots of light reaches the forest floor. So the little ones there can make lots of sugar in their leaves. Yes! They'll go to bed full of sweets.

But at some point, the first snow comes, and just like the big, brave trees, the little ones are no longer able to get rid of their leaves. The snow layer gets thicker and thicker until the small trees finally bend over.

Will it all work out okay? In the spring the snow melts, and the little trees straighten right up. Their thin trunks are so flexible that they're just fine. But as the years go by, the trunks of the tree children keep getting wider. Once the trunk is one to two inches (3–4 cm) across, things can get dangerous. If snow falls and bends the trunk now, the wood will crack. Ouch! That hurts. To make sure it doesn't happen again, the tree children start to drop their leaves each year, just like their mothers.

*

Trees can also show insects how brave they are by the color of their leaves in the fall. Bright leaves are a warning to insects. With these colors, the trees are saying, "Look here. I am strong and healthy. Lay your eggs somewhere else, because I can defend myself!"

This tree has kept its leaves too long in the autumn. Now it's bent over under the snow, and its branches may break off. Will this tree drop its leaves earlier next year?

TRY THIS!

IF YOU GO FOR A WALK in a forest near you in the fall, you can see for yourself all the different-colored leaves and notice which trees drop their leaves first. Which trees do you think are the bravest and strongest where you live?

WHICH TREES ARE RECORD HOLDERS?

Every tree is special and has its own unique qualities. Some are huge. Some are ancient. And some spread so far, a single tree can make a forest all by itself.

The scientist who discovered Old Tjikko named the ancient spruce for a dog he once owned. Old Tjikko may be ancient, but its trunk is only sixteen feet (5 m) tall.

MANY FORESTERS USED TO THINK that spruce trees could live to be up to five hundred years old. That's a long time, right? In forests managed for timber production, these conifers are usually cut down when they're about eighty years old (if they've managed to live that long without a storm knocking them over first). That's why no one paid much attention to a windswept spruce in Sweden. What could be so special about it?

But one day, scientists examined the small tree high up in the mountains more closely. To their amazement, they discovered that it was almost ten thousand years old! That's when they started to investigate other inconspicuous trees in the same area. And sure enough, they found a few more that were more than eight thousand years old.

The small spruce is called Old Tjikko. You can't visit it, because if too many tourists started to walk around it, its root system would be damaged. And nobody wants that. If it's left undisturbed, this tree may grow to be thousands of years older.

*

The tallest tree in the world isn't as old as Old Tjikko. Its name is Hyperion, and it's a coast redwood that grows on a steep hillside in California. At 380 feet (116 m), it's as tall as a big cathedral and very strong. But its roots are sensitive because they grow not far beneath the surface, and if tourists came to visit, they would cause damage with their shoes. (Imagine having lots of people treading on your toes every day!) So foresters don't reveal exactly where this tall tree stands.

*

Also in the United States, in Utah, there is a quaking aspen.

Just one? Not exactly—there are forty thousand trunks growing here. That would normally be nothing special, but this little forest has been given a name, Pando, because it's a single organism. It grows from one large root spread over an area of almost 106 acres (43 hectares)—about fifty city blocks in Manhattan. Every few yards, a trunk pushes out of the ground, looking as if it were a single tree.

So that raises the question: Is each trunk a single tree? Or is it part of a tree family? Scientists are still debating the answer, but I think it's a single tree, because the most important part of a tree is its roots. They make contact with neighboring trees and may even store memory. And just as your arms and legs are not your siblings, the different trunks of Pando are not separate trees. That's why Pando is probably the largest—that is to say the widest—tree in the world.

Quiz

Where do the smallest trees grow?

* **In the rainforest**
* **In Germany**
* **In Finland**

In Finland, in a remote part of the country called Lapland. The winters there are so long that trees hardly have any time to grow during the short summers. The birches and willows look like tiny shrubs and are sometimes no bigger than your hand.

TRY THIS!↑

DO YOU KNOW ANY RECORD-HOLDING TREES? You could try to find the trees in your town or in the nearest forest with the widest trunks. Simply measure how wide the trunks are using your arms. If the tree is so wide that your hands can't touch as they circle it, you'll need your family or friends to help. How many people does it take to hug the tree? If you want to know the exact measurement, use a tape measure. And if you like, take a photo and make a note of where that sturdy tree can be found.

Chapter 5

ANIMALS IN THE FOREST

EACH FOREST ANIMAL LIVES IN A different way. Some love living many floors up in a high-rise. Others prefer a damp basement. Some have phenomenal memories and others are expert farmers.

WHO LIVES WAY UP HIGH?

Some birds live in hollowed-out cavities in tree trunks. This has a lot of advantages. The tree's thick wooden walls keep them nice and warm all winter. And enemies can't get in very easily because the wood is so hard.

HOWEVER, HARDLY ANYONE CAN BUILD a tree house like this by themselves. One of the few animals that can handle tree trunks is the woodpecker. It has a strong, pointy beak that it uses to hack holes in the trees. Sometimes this works well, especially if the tree is already dead and rotten.

Wood rots when fungi extend their thin roots to slowly eat into the trunk. This makes the wood softer and softer. That's why smaller species of woodpeckers, such as the great spotted woodpecker in Europe and the downy woodpecker in North America, like to make their nest holes in dead trees. Their children will be safe because animals such as martens and squirrels can't get through the small opening. (Sometimes these animals will even try to grab the parents while they're sleeping inside, but the tree's wood protects the birds.)

Woodpeckers use tree cavities the same way you use your house, but rather than having all their rooms under one roof, they often build rooms in several different trees. That way they can choose where they want to sleep each night.

*

Large woodpeckers, such as the European black woodpecker, like to make their nest holes in thick, healthy beech trees. Beech wood is extremely hard, which makes the wood-peckers' cavities particularly sturdy and long-lasting.

But doesn't the woodpecker get a headache? After all, it has to hammer into the fresh, hard wood thousands of times with its beak. Don't worry—the woodpecker's brain is tucked into its head very firmly, so it doesn't wobble during all that tapping. Our brains, on the other hand, "float" in liquid inside our skulls. If we get a blow to the head, our brain bumps against the inside of our skull. And that hurts!

The woodpecker's beak is also attached with something like a rubber band, so when it hammers at the wood, its beak doesn't slam into its head with so much force.

Every scratch on the outside of a tree trunk resonates within, which makes it very difficult for animals such as martens to sneak up on whoever might have set up house inside the tree.

But hammering is still very hard work. That's why the woodpecker makes only a small hole in the trunk at first. Then it stops and waits a few months. During this time, fungi grow in the new hole, making the wood around the hole mushy and soft. Now the woodpecker can continue to work, and the job will be much easier.

A tree trunk acts like a kind of alarm system for a woodpecker. Sitting inside its cavity, it can hear every sound the tree makes. Sometimes these sounds are just branches creaking in the wind. But every now and then a marten climbs up the trunk, and its claws make soft, scratchy noises that sound quite loud inside the woodpecker's nest hole, giving it time to escape.

TRY THIS!

YOU AND A FRIEND CAN TRY out the woodpecker's forest early-warning system for yourself. Find a long tree trunk lying on the ground. While one person presses an ear against the thin end of the trunk, the other uses a small stone to tap or scratch on the thick end. The listener has to say whether the sound is scratching or tapping.

Look!

Community Housing

SOMETIMES A WOODPECKER WILL BUILD several holes, one above the other. Then its home looks like a high-rise with several floors—or perhaps like a giant wooden flute. If the edges of the holes are light in color, you'll know that the woodpecker was working there just a short while ago. When the woodpecker no longer needs the dwelling, other animals that can't build their own holes can move right in. Bats, doves, and owls are happy to take up residence in these forest high-rises. That's why it's important not to cut these trees down, even if they're dead—they still have a special role to play in the forest as animal homes.

WHO CAN FIT INTO A LEAF?

There are all sorts of animals in the forest, and most of them are tiny. The tiny ones can look for smaller homes than larger animals—much smaller homes!

Leaf-mining larvae leave distinctive tracks as they snack their way through leaves.

BECAUSE SMALL ANIMALS ARE EATEN by large animals, they like their homes to have walls so that others can't get in easily.

The beech leaf-mining weevil (funny name, right?) looks for homes just like this. This small beetle likes to live in beech trees. It's an odd-looking creature. Its mouth looks like an elephant's trunk, and it's an excellent jumper. If a bird comes to eat it, it simply springs away. But its babies, the larvae, can't do that yet. They look like little worms and have to eat leaves for weeks before they can turn into beetles, because this transformation takes a lot of energy.

*

The small larvae live dangerously. There are lots of birds that love to eat them. That's why they hide inside the leaves.

But how can they do this? A beech leaf is pretty thin!

The beetle mothers lay their eggs right on the leaf, and the larvae take care of the rest. Because they're so tiny when they hatch, they can simply eat their way into the leaf.

*

Over the weeks, as they get bigger, they continue to feed themselves by tunneling their way through the inside of the leaf. That's why this beetle is called a "miner."

You can see their work when you look at the leaf from the outside. The larvae leave a thin brown line behind them. It's wavy because the beetle children don't move in a straight line but wander around as they're feeding. The line gets wider as the larvae get fatter.

Finally, the larvae take a rest and turn into beetles. The beetles crawl out of the leaf and are hungry right away, so they eat lots of small holes in the fresh leaves. You can see these holes easily if you hold a leaf up against the light.

*

Other beetles, such as bark beetles, do something similar. Bark is the outside layer of a tree, and that's where these beetles lay their eggs—hence their name. The larvae can then easily eat their way under the bark so they can't be seen from the outside.

Unfortunately, this isn't very nice for the trees, because the bark is their skin! And when many larvae start nibbling away, the tree dies. But this only happens if the tree is already sick. A healthy tree can defend itself against the beetles. It pumps poison into its leaves or bark, and the beetles lose their appetite.

Mostly it's spruce trees that are visited by bark beetles. Healthy spruces simply pump out a bit of pitch as a beetle drills holes Into the bark. Then the beetle is stuck there and can't do any more damage.

*

By the way, it's not so bad for beech trees when leaf-mining weevils nibble on them, because they only munch on parts of the leaves—they don't eat them all up. Even if larvae are living there, the tree can still use its leaves. So the beetle babies don't actually bother the tree too much.

TRY THIS!

FIND OUT FOR YOURSELF HOW STICKY pitch can be. Find a conifer with drops of pitch on the trunk. Try sticking on small stones or twigs. Make a face using two pebbles for eyes, a small twig as a nose, and a mouth of small stones. If the pitch isn't in the right place, take a stick and smear it where you need it. Don't touch it with your fingers, though. It's very difficult to clean pitch off your hands—and your clothes!

Look!

Bark Beetles

IF YOU FIND A DEAD CONIFER, you can examine its bark for evidence of beetles. Want to know how to recognize a dead conifer? It's pretty easy: the bark is falling off, and there are no longer needles on the branches, though there may be some beneath the tree.

Take a piece of bark from one of these trees. You'll probably see that bark beetles have been eating here. You can tell by the lines that spread out from one spot, a bit like a star. Each line comes from a larva that has eaten here. Sometimes in the autumn there are still young beetles in the bark. They're waiting, nice and protected, for the coming spring.

WHO'S THE BEST FOREST DETECTIVE?

If forest animals don't want to starve in the winter, they need to stock up on food ahead of time. That's why jays take care to hide thousands of tidbits in the soil every autumn. And any seeds they don't eat have a chance to grow into new trees.

EVEN THOUGH THE BRAIN OF A JAY is fairly small and works very differently from ours, this bird is really smart. It's able to remember each place where it has hidden food, and exactly what it has buried there. Acorns and beechnuts remain fresh for more than six months, while dead earthworms only last a few days. The bird knows it has to eat the worms first so they don't spoil. That's pretty clever, isn't it?

Not only that, but the jay keeps an eye out in case another jay is watching it bury its food, so it can steal it. (Yes, birds will do such a thing!) And then, of course, it has to remember exactly where each hiding place is. After all, it has to be able to find the food again when everything is under a thick layer of snow in the winter.

You can sometimes catch a jay doing this. If it's hungry, it will fly in to land and, bingo, with only a single peck in the ground, the food is instantly found. It can remember up to ten thousand hiding places. The bird doesn't really need that many—usually, two thousand acorns and beechnuts are enough to see it through the winter. But because the jay can't be sure that will be enough, it prefers to bury a few thousand more just in case.

This is great for the forest because in the spring, a small tree will sprout from every beechnut and acorn that the bird didn't need. That's why jays are so popular with foresters. They help to create new forests, and it doesn't cost a cent!

*

The Eurasian jay is a bird with a phenomenal memory.

The squirrel does the same thing. It also collects a lot of tree seeds in the fall and buries them as a winter supply. But unlike the jay, it only collects as many seeds as it really needs. The problem is that the squirrel is quite forgetful and often can't remember exactly where its hiding places are.

You can see this happening in the winter. The squirrel digs a bit here, digs a bit there. Then it sits down and thinks, *Where did I put those acorns again?*

A squirrel buries several nuts in one hole but often forgets exactly where it has stashed them.

It doesn't remember all the hiding places. That's why, unfortunately, many squirrels don't survive the winter.

You can sometimes see their forgotten hiding places in the spring. Small bunches of beech and oak trees will grow where a squirrel once buried several seeds together in a hole. At most one of these tree seedlings will survive the next few years.

*

There's a third member of this seed-collecting gang. The wood mouse also carries many seeds at the same time, but usually hides its loot in a hollow tree. Here the mouse can eat in peace, without being discovered by a fox. But when this happens, it doesn't help the beechnuts. They won't sprout in the spring because they get no light or water inside the hollow tree.

Look!

Guardians of the Forest

CROWS HELP FORESTS SPREAD, NOT ONLY because they carry seeds away but also because they test the seeds before they hide them to make sure they're firm and fresh. Because crows gather seeds from a wide area, the new forests they plant are full of different kinds of trees, which helps give the forests a healthy start. The trees best adapted to their new environment will grow strong and tall.

Quiz

If trees voted for the best animal to collect and bury their seeds, who would they choose?

* Squirrel
* Wood mouse
* Jay

Jay. The seeds buried by squirrels often have too little space to grow, and the seeds hidden by wood mice receive too little light to start growing at all.

ARE THERE FARMERS IN THE FOREST, TOO?

I'm not talking about human farmers. We humans do farm many kinds of animals—cows, horses, goats—usually out in open, green fields. But did you know that there are tiny animals that tend to their livestock up in the green leaves of trees?

TREES DON'T LIKE APHIDS, WHICH SUCK the sugar juice out of their leaves—sugar that the hungry trees made for themselves to use. The aphids waste a lot of this precious liquid. They drink so much that most of it comes out in their pee and falls from the tree. When cars are parked under trees infested with aphids, they quickly become covered with sticky droplets. (Take a look at the windshields the next time you walk down a tree-lined street in the summer!)

Ants love sugar juice, too. That's why they like to climb trees where aphids suck. They like the juice so much that they drink it straight from the rear ends of the aphids. Doesn't sound too appetizing, does it? But with aphids, what's coming out is basically just

water and sugar. That's why the droplets are clear and not yellow like pee.

If the ants are very hungry, they don't wait for the juice to come out. They'll milk the aphids, like a farmer milks cows. The ants tap on the aphids' rear ends with their antennae to make them squeeze out a drop of sugar water—called honeydew. The ants suck it up and carry the honeydew back home to the big anthill where they all live. There, they pass it on to other ants so that everyone has their fill.

*

A farmer who keeps cows needs a fence, because without one, the herd would just wander off. Ants have a similar problem with aphids. But they can't build a fence with posts and wire. They keep their small herd of aphids together in a different way.

Mostly aphids sit on the undersides of leaves, where they can feed without getting wet. To keep them corralled, ants have come up with two tricks. Sometimes aphids grow wings so they can fly away. The ants simply bite off their wings.

But the aphids could still run away, couldn't they? After all, they still have legs.

Don't worry—the ants don't bite their legs off. Instead, they run around the aphids, leaving a strange scent that makes the aphids dizzy and drowsy. After that, the aphids move more slowly and no longer want to leave. It's almost as if they were drunk.

*

Even though they're being held captive, the aphids don't have a bad life. They just sit on the leaves and do what they love best: drink sugar juice. They're well protected, too. Their enemies, ladybugs, can't attack them,

An ant defends its aphids by attacking a ladybug.

because the ants are keeping watch. As soon as a ladybug approaches, the ants drive it away. So the aphids live in peace and without fear.

TRY THIS!

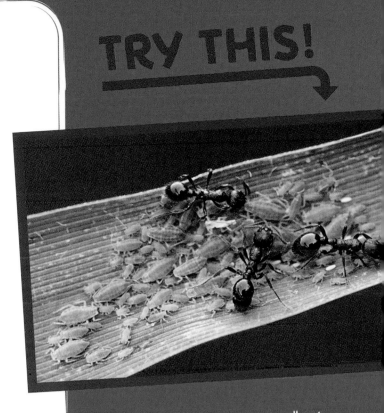

IF YOU WANT TO SEE HOW well ants watch over their herds of aphids, take a blade of grass. Now look for a leaf that has a small bunch of aphids on its underside. Are there also ants running around on the branches? If so, that's perfect. If you tickle the aphids with the blade of grass, the ants will come running to defend the aphids. They will rear up on their hind legs as if to say, "Get lost!" Sometimes they'll even bite into the blade of grass, thinking it's an attacking animal.

Quiz

Forest honey is especially delicious. What do bees make it from?

* **The nectar of forest flowers**
* **Aphid pee**

Aphid pee. Honey is simply sugar water bees have sucked up and spat out back in the hive. They make flower honey from flower nectar and forest honey from aphid honeydew.

Chapter 6

TREES ARE AWESOME

TREES GROWING TOGETHER IN THE
forest can do some amazing things.
They can make us feel happier and
more relaxed, and they can make
our planet a more pleasant
and healthier place to live. But,
unfortunately, we don't always
make things easy for them.

CAN FORESTS MAKE IT RAIN?

Everything gets thirsty in the summer. Trees, and people, too.
When it doesn't rain for a long time, it would be very useful to be
able to make the rain yourself. And some trees can do just that.

When it rains, water vapor often rises above the trees and forms new clouds.

BECAUSE WATER IS SO MOBILE and always wants to go downward, rainwater tends to soak into the ground or flow downhill. At some point the rainwater that runs downhill gathers in streams and rivers. In time, they carry the water to the sea.

If there were no rain supply from above, things would dry out quickly on land, and you would soon be living in a desert. Fortunately, heavy rain clouds gather all the time. They form over the sea, where the water vapor rises from below and collects in clouds. The wind blows these clouds to us on land, where the moisture falls out as rain or snow. At some point the clouds disappear and the sky is blue again.

But what about places so far from the sea that clouds don't reach them because they've already released all their water? These places aren't necessarily dry. If there are big forests between these places and the sea, the trees can make new clouds after it rains.

It works like this. Look out a window with a view of a forest or park. After a big summer thunderstorm, you'll see dense plumes of water vapor rise above the trees. It almost looks like smoke. This vapor rises high in the sky and forms clouds.

The same thing happens in a forest that stands near the sea. When it rains, water vapor will rise over the forest, and new clouds will form and travel on the wind inland, where it rains again. And if there's a forest there, too, then after the rain, new clouds will form, which the wind will drive even farther inland. And so it goes on and on, from forest to forest.

That's how the rain reaches places that are more than a thousand miles away from the closest ocean. Scientists have only learned about this recently. When the rainforest in the middle of Brazil started to dry up, they realized that it had something to do with the forests by the sea, which people had cut down. Now they're trying to let these forests grow back again.

*

*

In Russia, forests make rain quite differently: they summon up the clouds.

There are huge spruce forests here. It's very cold in the winter, but in summer it can be very hot and dry. The spruces don't like that, so they create clouds from scratch to help themselves.

They do this by exhaling from their needles tiny droplets that smell spicy-sweet, like the pitch they pump out of their trunks to defend themselves from beetles. These droplets rise up into the air and collect water. The droplets become larger drops and gather together to form clouds. Eventually the drops become so heavy that the clouds can no longer hold them, and they fall to the ground as rain!

In this way, spruce trees can produce clouds and rain themselves. And the clouds provide another advantage: they act like a parasol that shields the forest from the sun, making it shadier and cooler.

TRY THIS!

FIND A THICK DEAD TREE TRUNK in the forest, preferably one that's nice and rotten, with very soft wood, so that if you press down firmly with your finger, a bit of water will come out. See if that also works on a hot, dry summer day— usually it will. You've found the forest's air-conditioning!

Look!

Seeking Shelter

MANY CONIFERS COME FROM PLACES where it's cool and wet. Their crowns are narrow and their branches hang down, which makes the trees look a bit like giant, partially opened umbrellas. And, indeed, you can use them like an umbrella. If you're out for a walk and it starts to rain, look to see if there's a spruce or fir tree nearby. Its branches will protect you from the rain, and you'll stay nice and dry until the shower has passed.

HOW DO FORESTS CLEAN WATER?

Raindrops can pack quite a punch. The fatter the drops, the harder they hit the ground. With every drop a little bit of earth shoots up, and with many drops this can amount to a lot of soil on the move.

DURING A THUNDERSTORM, THE GROUND QUICKLY turns to mud. Rainwater flushes this muddy soup into the nearest stream. That's not good for the ground: over time the layer of soil will become thinner and thinner. This may happen so slowly that at first you barely even notice it.

How quickly the soil disappears depends on what's growing in the ground. On a farm field, you see a lot of exposed soil because it's dug up each year. In the autumn the farmer harvests everything, and by winter the field lies brown and bare. During the winter, raindrops can hit the ground directly and wash away a lot of soil. In a hundred years, twenty inches (50 cm) of soil can disappear. That doesn't sound like much—a hundred years is a long time—but you can't bring back the soil that has been washed away. Soon you'll see many stones that used to be hidden beneath the surface poking out of the ground. Without a layer of soil covering the stones, very little will now grow here.

*

If a lot of rain comes down at once and the water runs off the field quickly, the plants growing there have another problem. There's hardly any time for the water to soak down to their roots, so they have very little to drink.

Things are very different where a group of trees is growing together. The fat raindrops splash down onto their leaves. This doesn't bother the leaves. They happily bounce back when each drop hits, and the water then runs slowly along the branches to the trunk and down to the ground. Drops also often fall directly off the leaves, but these drops aren't as fat and heavy as they were before. They don't smash against the ground but land softly on leaves below and on moss on the forest floor.

From here the water seeps very slowly into the ground. That way it doesn't flow into the nearest stream, and no soil is washed away.

*

The trees need to drink some of this water, and they suck it up with their roots. The rest slowly soaks deeper into the ground—sometimes 150 feet (50 m), sometimes many hundreds more. Deep below the surface, the water collects and forms large underground lakes and rivers.

Many years pass before the water reaches this point. Any dirt in the rainwater, such as animal excrement or soot, stays trapped in the soil and in the rocks below it. This makes the deep groundwater so clean that you can drink it.

But first it must be hauled up. That's what waterworks are for, with their big pumps. They suck the water out of the ground through pipes and fill tanks with it. From there it flows through more pipes straight into your house. All you have to do is turn on the tap.

*

So the water you drink at home might have originally been forest water. If there's no forest near your water station, then the water has seeped through farmland, or it comes from lakes or rivers. This kind of water has to be cleaned before it can be used, because it hasn't already been cleaned by the forest. That costs a lot of money, and the water doesn't always taste so good, either. So it's much easier to allow enough forests to grow. The trees help us for free!

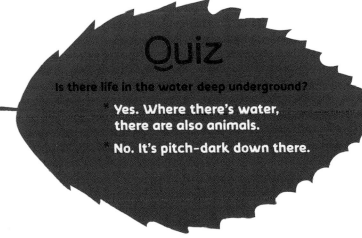

Quiz

Is there life in the water deep underground?

* **Yes. Where there's water, there are also animals.**

* **No. It's pitch-dark down there.**

Yes. There are indeed animals deep underground—small crustaceans, for example. They are blind because there's no light down there, and animals that live in constant darkness have no need for eyes. These crustaceans can only live in very clean water. That's why they especially like it when a forest grows above them.

TRY THIS!

YOU CAN BUILD YOUR OWN WATER filter. First, you'll need a bucket with holes in the bottom. Layer stones and soil on the bottom to make a miniature farm field. Now you just need a bit of dirty water. Stir a little soil into a glass of water and pour the cloudy water into the bucket. Look at what comes out of the bottom: it's still dirty.

Now empty the bucket and do the same thing, but this time make a miniature forest floor. Put some stones in the bottom of the bucket, then a bit of leaf mold. (Dig deep into the decaying leaves on the ground and take some brown, crumbly stuff along with the leaves.) Carefully place a layer of moss on top of this.

Now pour dirty water into the bucket again. If everything works properly, the water will be much cleaner when it comes out of the bottom. The forest works just like this!

WHY ARE TREES IMPORTANT IN THE CITY?

A city looks nicer when trees grow there. But for trees, life in the city, with all its traffic and buildings, isn't always that easy. Nevertheless, it's important that trees live here, too.

Trees cool cities down and make them more beautiful.

WHEN TREES GROW, THEY PRODUCE OXYGEN. This is the most important part of the air for us humans. A single large tree produces enough oxygen for twenty people to breathe.

And that's not all. With its leaves or needles, a tree collects a lot of dirt out of the air, such as the soot that comes from car exhaust pipes or from chimneys. Each tree can collect more than a thousand pounds (500 kg) of soot per year. All this dirt is trapped in the treetops and washed out onto the ground with the next rain. That's a good thing for the tree—otherwise it would no longer be able to make sugar because the sunlight can't reach the surface of leaves that are covered in soot.

*

As you learned earlier in this book, trees talk to and warn each other, and they even talk to animals using a scent language. You can smell that scent. You may not notice it, but your body will. If you walk under trees a lot, you'll feel better.

Looking at trees is good for you, too. Sometimes if you're sick in bed, it's enough just to look at a tree—you'll get well faster. Researchers in hospitals have discovered as much. That's why it's good to plant as many trees as possible in cities.

Urban trees are also important for the climate. In the heat of summer, trees create cooler air in the city, the same way they do in the forest.

*

Nevertheless, some people get annoyed by the trees that line city streets. The leaves that fall on the sidewalks in the fall must be swept up. The treetops cast shadows on houses and gardens. During storms, branches can break off and fall on people or cars.

For all these reasons, the trees are pruned. Arborists, who understand how trees work and grow, trim them very carefully. They saw a little here and cut a little there, and you barely notice that a few branches are missing. Afterward, people can walk under the tree safely and the tree remains healthy.

*

But there's another reason trees are so important. They're fun! In a way they're a bit like elephants: huge, only much slower. If you're lucky, you can even watch them from your window. Then you can see how they behave over the course of a year and how they change with time. You can be a naturalist without leaving your room.

Of course, it's better to go out and visit the trees in person. And you can even pet them, unlike elephants. Whether they'll notice has yet to be investigated, but you never know...

TRY THIS!

FIND OUT HOW MANY DIFFERENT TREES grow in your neighborhood. Take a leaf or needle from each tree and place it between the pages of a newspaper. Now stack heavy books on top. After a few days, the leaves will be dry and completely flat, and you can glue them onto a piece of paper. They'll keep like this for several years. Use a guidebook or the internet to see which kinds of trees you've found.

Look!

Moss and More

IF YOU STAND RIGHT IN FRONT of a tree, you'll see all sorts of other living things growing on the bark. Moss, for example, loves the water that runs down the trunk when it rains. That's why it grows there.

Sometimes the bark appears so red, it looks rusted. That's because of algae—tiny plants that live on the tree trunk, like moss does.

Green or gray spots are lichens, which are a mix of algae and fungi. They grow very slowly and always need something to cling to.

None of these plants harm the tree at all.

DO TREES SLEEP AT NIGHT?

Have you ever wondered what trees do at night? Spending a day in the sun is quite exhausting, and by the evening, trees, just like humans, are really tired. And, like us, they need to sleep so they'll be in shape the next morning.

These trees would like to go to sleep, but how can they do that when the lights are on?

SCIENTISTS HAVE MEASURED SLEEPING TREES. They've noticed that when trees sleep, their branches hang down a bit. When it gets light, the branches perk up again. It's as though the trees wake up when the sun rises.

Researchers don't yet know what trees do when they're asleep. They were completely surprised to learn that trees go to sleep in the first place. There's still a great deal to find out. Maybe you'll be the one to discover whether trees dream!

At night trees can't produce oxygen. This important part of the air that we need to breathe is produced when the leaves make sugar. But that only happens with light. The sun doesn't shine at night, so the trees do the same thing we do: they take a break.

When you sleep, you still have to breathe. You consume the air in your room—or, more precisely, the oxygen in it—and as a result the air in your bedroom gets a bit worse overnight. So it's good to open the window in the morning to let in some fresh air.

It's no different in the forest. The air gets a bit worse at night because the trees continue to breathe and consume oxygen just like we do. There are no windows in the forest, but it doesn't matter, because as soon as the sun shines in the morning, the leaves start to make sugar again, and more oxygen is produced.

*

The air in the forest is always better than the air in your room because trees don't consume much oxygen at night. In addition—where I live, anyway—the wind from the west brings a lot of fresh air from the sea. And because many small plants called algae live in the sea and produce oxygen in the seawater, there's plenty of oxygen to breathe everywhere, even inside.

*

If we wanted to make things easier for city trees, we wouldn't turn on so many lights at night. Trees especially don't like streetlights that stay on all night. Can you imagine trying to sleep with the lights turned on? You would probably have bad dreams and still be tired in the morning. Trees aren't that different, and when they grow next to streetlights, they don't grow to be very old.

But a city without light isn't good, either, because then you wouldn't be able to see anything when you're walking down the sidewalk at night.

Maybe trees and people could cooperate. The streetlights could stay on until midnight, and after that they would turn off. By then most people would be home in bed, and the trees on the street could sleep.

Look!

Turn Down the Lights

IT'S ALSO BETTER FOR MANY ANIMALS if there's no artificial light at night. Moths, for example, always look for the moon so they know which direction to fly. But they don't know about streetlights, and they mistake them for actual moons. Confused, they fly around the lights in circles until they fall to the ground, exhausted. One way you can make life easier for night-flying insects is to talk to your parents about turning off unnecessary lights outside your house or installing motion-detector lights, which light up only when they're needed and give animals—and trees!—the darkness they enjoy when people aren't around.

Chapter 7

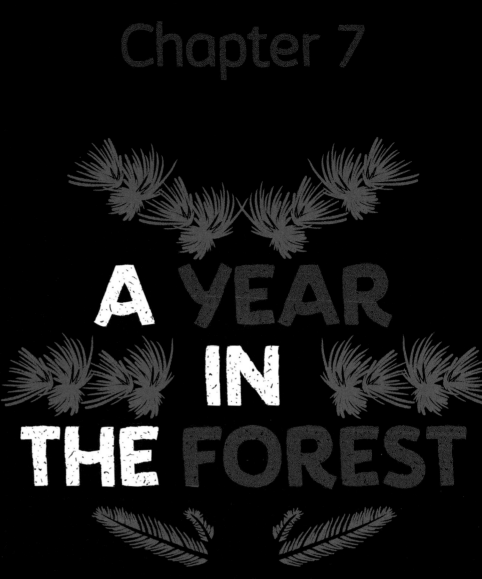

A YEAR IN THE FOREST

IN THE SPRING THE LEAVES UNFURL, and birds start to build their nests. During the hot summer, animals and people enjoy the cool forest air. In autumn the leaves of the forest change color. And in the winter the forest grows quiet while all the animals are dozing.

HOW DO TREES KNOW WHEN IT'S SPRING?

As it warms up in spring, trees awake from their winter sleep. First they pump water into their trunks. Then they get ready to grow their leaves. But what wakes them up?

TREES ARE WOKEN UP BY THEIR mothers. But they wake up much more slowly than you do. This can take many days.

First they realize that it's getting warmer. They feel this much the same way you do. Then they see that the sun is rising a bit earlier each day and going down later. (Yes, trees really can "see" a little, probably through the scales on their buds, which act like little windows. The scales are almost transparent, so they let sunbeams through to the leaves. The leaves lie folded up inside the buds, but they're already green and ready to start work.)

Beech trees, for example, have something like an internal clock. They wait until it's light for at least thirteen hours a day. Then they know that it really is spring, and they begin to unfurl their leaves. If they were to start doing this too early in the year, a strong frost could come and freeze the delicate little leaves.

Apple trees take things especially carefully. Before they leaf out, they count the number of warm days that reach 68 degrees Fahrenheit (20°C).

Count? Yes, you read that right. Only after a certain number of days have been reached are the trees sure that it's truly spring, and that they can safely wake up.

It's different with conifers. Except for the larch, dawn redwood, and bald cypress, conifers keep their narrow, pointed leaves on their branches all winter.

Because conifers stay green year-round, they get to work quickly once they wake up in the spring. Spruce trees will even start when it's still freezing.

*

As soon as their leaves have grown, the trees begin to capture sunlight and make sugar. But the tender new leaves taste good to many animals. Trees have to watch out for the caterpillars of a particular small moth nibbling on their leaves. Sometimes so many are sitting in the treetops at once that it's actually noisy.

Baby birds are always hungry! Their parents feed them the caterpillars that they find on trees. That's good for the trees and good for the chicks.

The noise doesn't come from the wind, but from the caterpillars themselves. Millions of caterpillars are eating and pooping at the same time, and their droppings fall to the ground as tiny black pellets. It sounds like a heavy rainfall.

When so many of these caterpillars attack the leaves (happily this only happens every ten to twenty years), the trees can be eaten bare by June. But most trees are strong enough to leaf out again. And once the caterpillar plague is over, they can grow undisturbed for the rest of the summer.

*

For animals, too, this is the beginning of a lovely time of year. Creatures that have been hibernating wake up, and babies are born. Mothers have plenty of milk for their offspring, because juicy plants are everywhere, and they can quickly eat their fill. Birds hatch chicks and feed them the caterpillars that are munching on the spring leaves.

The temperature has gone up, too. Everyone is warm and well fed and with their families. Animal children like this as much as you do!

TRY THIS! ⤴

IN THE SPRINGTIME, YOU WOULDN'T starve to death in the forest—you can make a salad from young birch leaves. They're very tender and taste a bit sour. Please take only the lower leaves of big trees—they're not that important to the tree because they don't get much light anyway. You can also eat the fresh, light-green growing tips at the ends of spruce branches, although they may still be tart and a little bitter. You can make tea from them—they taste best that way. (But only taste leaves if you have an adult with you who can positively identify the tree species, as not all are edible and some are poisonous.)

Wildflowers bloom in early spring, before the trees leaf out and shut off the light.

Quiz

How many leaves does a mature deciduous tree grow every spring?

* **More than one thousand**
* **About five thousand**
* **At least fifty thousand**

A mature deciduous tree has at least fifty thousand leaves, and it could have as many as a hundred thousand.

DO TREES SWEAT IN SUMMER?

Summer is also a good time for trees. The days are long now, and the sun is high in the sky at noon. That means the trees have lots of light.

WITH SO MUCH LIGHT, TREES CAN make lots of sugar, so they never go hungry in the summer. On the contrary, by July or August they've already stored enough sugar for the following winter. Trees are much like bears this way. During the summer, bears eat as much grass and as many berries and fish as they can find. This makes them big and fat. They store the fat under their skin, and this helps keep them from starving as they sleep through the winter. So trees and bears are similar, at least when it comes to gathering and storing food.

If the trees have flowered in the spring, then by summer, green fruit and seeds are hanging from every branch. The tree is gradually getting bigger, and this uses up much of its energy. The beechnuts, acorns, and other seeds also contain a lot of fat and sugar, which the trees will no longer have for their winter supply. And then there's the fact that all those flowers and seeds are taking up space where leaves would normally be. It's crowded up there!

Having fewer leaves also means the trees aren't able to make as much sugar. If the trees have seeds, they have less sugar for themselves to use and to store for the winter, and that makes them weaker. That's why some species, such as beech or oak, will take a break from flowering over the next few years—to give themselves time to recover.

*

Sometimes trees can also get too hot. That's when beech trees, for example, will all sweat at the same time. You probably know how sweating works. You sweat, and as the film of water evaporates from your skin, you cool down. But beech trees don't sweat through their skin—they release water through their

By summer, young great horned owls have learned to hunt for themselves.

leaves. This makes the air more humid, and the forest temperature cools by several degrees. For the people and animals in the forest, this feels pretty good on hot days!

*

For animal children, summer is the best season. It's warm and mostly dry, and there's enough to eat and drink. Deer and squirrel mothers have plenty of milk, and bird parents bring in huge amounts of insects to keep their chicks satisfied.

Childhood lasts only a year for most animals, so this is when they must learn a lot from their parents. But there's also time to have fun. You may see young foxes at play—and not paying proper attention. They may run onto the road during a game of tag and then freeze when a car comes along. That's pretty dangerous!

*

Many smaller animals don't like the sun. Salamanders, for instance, hide under rotting wood and come out only after dark or after it has rained so their sensitive skin doesn't dry out. The spotted salamander, found in the eastern United States and Canada, has algae in cells inside its body that produce oxygen, much like a tree makes oxygen in its leaves.

TRY THIS!

YOU CAN FEEL FOR YOURSELF how much trees cool the forest when they sweat. On a hot summer day, notice how the temperature changes as soon as you go from a treeless landscape into the forest. It's shady beneath the trees and much more humid, which can make it more than eighteen degrees Fahrenheit (10°C) cooler than outside the forest. A good place to take a break!

And here's another good thing: there are no horseflies or deerflies in the shade. These are large biting flies that, like mosquitoes, like to drink blood, and their bites really hurt. They're the main reason many animals seek out shade in the summer.

WHY DO TREES SHED THEIR LEAVES IN FALL?

Autumn is the time when trees and animals prepare for winter. The animals eat lots once again. They want to make themselves nice and fat because in winter there will be little food around.

ANIMALS CAN FIND PLENTY TO EAT when the beeches and oaks are loaded with fruit. Beechnuts and acorns fill them up quickly, but these nuts only mature every few years. In between, forest animals and birds must make do with other fruits and plants.

Deer especially need a lot of food in autumn, because that's when their mating season begins. In some species, the male deer roar through the night until they're hoarse to chase away other males that are competing for the females. They spend so much time bellowing that they don't eat, and after a few weeks they're very thin. It's all very exhausting and hot work (think of how you feel after playing sports for a long time), so they only do this when it gets really cold.

*

The trees also sense that it's become colder. They can see with their buds and leaves that the days are getting shorter. Now it's time to drop their foliage, because if they keep their leaves, more snow can

The fiery colors of fall show that trees are preparing to shut down for their winter break.

gather on their branches. The branches would become very heavy and could break under the weight of a heavy snowfall.

But, as we've seen in Chapter 4, trees can only drop their leaves when they're awake, just like you can't take off your clothes when you're sleeping. And trees fall asleep as soon as there's a hard frost, whether they want to or not. So they have to pay close attention to the approach of winter and cold temperatures. As a precaution, they usually decide to drop their leaves in the last two weeks of October. Among conifers, only the larch, dawn redwood, and bald cypress drop their needles. All the others, such as spruce or pine, keep their needles and store a kind of natural antifreeze to prevent the needles from freezing.

*

When deciduous trees discard their leaves, they use that as a chance to get rid of waste—the tree version of going to the toilet. Yes, trees do it, too. They simply pump substances that they want to get rid of into their foliage. Only then do they let their leaves fall.

Does once a year seem like too little? Well, trees do things very slowly, so that's enough for them. Conifers also "go to the toilet" in the fall. But because they only lose a small portion of their oldest needles, it's barely noticeable.

*

Many birds in northern forests fly south in early autumn to places where it's warmer and there's more to eat. They learn how to get there from their parents. Other species stay put, although it gets very cold. Because they no longer have chicks to feed, they can get along on whatever food they can find. And they don't have to risk the long and dangerous flight to warmer places.

TRY THIS!

COLLECT LEAVES THAT ARE TURNING color. Cut them into tiny pieces and put a small handful into an old jam jar. (Use different jars for different-colored leaves.) Pour in just enough white vinegar to cover the leaves, then mash them up using the handle of an old wooden spoon. Cover the jars with plastic wrap, put them in a bowl of hot water, and leave them for half an hour. Cut a paper towel into long, narrow strips. Take the jars out of the bowl and remove the plastic wrap. Drape the strips over the edges of the jars so just the tip of the towel touches the liquid. After a few hours, remove the strips and allow them to dry overnight. In the morning, check the strips to see what colors have been revealed.

WHAT'S THERE TO EAT IN THE FOREST IN WINTER?

In the winter it's much brighter in the forest than it is in the summer, and it's almost silent. The birds seldom call, and the big animals are feeling lazy and tired.

A lynx with its sights set on snowshoe hare for dinner.

TIRED ANIMALS ARE SLOW, AND THOSE that don't move much don't need to eat so much. That's why deer spend so much time standing around and dozing in the winter. They hardly find anything to eat in the forest. The grasses and plants have dried up, and most of the shrubs have shed their leaves. All that remain are buds, bark, and the leaves of plants like the blackberry, which keeps its green foliage even in winter.

All of this together is barely enough to keep the animals from starving. That isn't a problem for carnivores like the fox, wolf, and marten, because the animals they hunt are still around in the winter, so they can find enough to eat.

Some animals, such as hedgehogs and bears, live very frugally at this time. They just sleep through the whole winter and don't eat anything more. Their bodies get what they need from the layer of fat under their skin.

*

The trees, too, are now in deep hibernation. They continue to breathe, bringing in air through their bark and roots. They need energy to do this—the sugar they made and stored beneath their bark and in their roots during the summer. But this supply is slowly being used up, and the trees have to ration what remains. After all, they need enough energy to survive until the spring and have some left to grow new leaves.

Sometimes there's a warm spell in the middle of winter. Then the snow melts, and you might think that spring has come. When this happens, it's important that the trees don't think winter is over. Because if they start to form new leaves now, they'll lose them

A snowy day is a great time to get out into the forest to see which creatures have been scurrying around despite the cold. What stories will their tracks tell?

IF YOU TAKE A WALK IN a coniferous forest after it has snowed heavily, you'll see that the snow-covered branches are folded down on top of each other like tiles on a roof. This is how the trees protect themselves. Each layer of branches supports the layer above so they don't break under the heavy load.

in the next severe frost. And that can happen even in April. But you already know that trees pay close attention and count the hours or days so they know for sure when it's truly spring again.

*

It's frequently very stormy during the winter, and that's when you can see which trees are well anchored in the ground. Often at this time the ground is soft and wet, so the roots have a poor grip. Large conifers with shallow root systems fall over particularly easily. That happens especially with trees that have been planted as seedlings to be grown for their timber. During planting the sensitive roots are often damaged, so they never grow properly and they can't hold onto the ground well.

This doesn't happen to deciduous trees as easily. They mostly grow from seeds, and so their roots penetrate deep into the soil. In addition, they have no leaves on their branches in winter. The wind whistles through the bare canopy and can't topple the trees.

*

For trees and animals, lots of snow is a good thing. The snow acts like a warm blanket, protecting the ground from freezing too deeply. This is especially good for small animals that can't dig too far down, because it means they'll still be well protected. When the snow melts, the meltwater slowly soaks into the ground, where it forms a large reservoir for the summer, so the trees will have enough to drink.

PHOTO CREDITS

39 left baobab © David Thyberg / Shutterstock.com; **right** cannonball flower © SvitlanaBelinska / iStockphoto.com

40 snow on trees © coophil / iStockphoto.com

41 snow on green tree © rsooll / iStockphoto.com

42 Old Tjikko, Sweden © Peter Wohlleben

43 girls hugging tree © sirtravelalot / Shutterstock.com

44–45 Northern flicker © FRANKHILDEBRAND / iStockphoto.com

46 pine marten © PhotocechCZ / Shutterstock.com

47 left girl listening to log © Jens Steingässer; **right** woodpecker holes © Antonia Banyard

48 leaf-mining larvae tracks © blickwinkel / Alamy Stock Photo

49 left bark beetle © Henrik Larsson / Shutterstock.com; **right** bark beetle lines © wjarek / Shutterstock.com

50 western scrub jay © Voodison328 / Shutterstock.com

51 left squirrel © Argument / iStockphoto.com; **right** crow © Sandra Standbridge / Shutterstock.com

52 aphid © Gerd Guenther / Science Photo Library

53 top ants and aphids © hekakoskinen / iStockphoto.com; **bottom** ants and ladybug © maldesowhat / iStockphoto.com

54–55 two boys on logs © woolzian / iStockphoto.com

56 misty forest © Mordolff / iStockphoto.com

57 left dead tree trunk © ifish / iStockphoto.com; **right** umbrella-shaped tree © Nosyrevy / Shutterstock.com

58 rain on leaves © olaser / iStockphoto.com

59 moss in bucket © Jens Steingässer

60 city playground © Marina113 / iStockphoto.com

61 left girl climbing tree © Purino / Shutterstock.com; **right** lichen on trunk © F-Stop boy / Shutterstock.com

62 park at night © cmart7327 / iStockphoto.com

63 streetlights © kunakos / iStockphoto.com

64–65 winter sunset © sborisov / iStockphoto.com

66 leaf buds © miss_j / iStockphoto.com

67 top left chicks in nest © LARISA SHPINEVA / iStockphoto.com; **top right** spruce tips © Artreef / Shutterstock.com; **bottom** wildflowers © symbiot / Shutterstock.com

68 fox kits © codyhoagland / Shutterstock.com

69 top left great horned owl juveniles © Alan Vernon. Used with permission; **top right** children in forest © Bosnian / Shutterstock.com; **bottom** spotted salamander © JasonOndreicka / iStockphoto.com

70 forest in fall colors © DieterMeyrl / iStockphoto.com

71 top left elk © Glass and Nature / Shutterstock.com; **top and bottom right** fall leaves, paper strips with leaves © Antonia Banyard

72 lynx © Action Sports Photography / Shutterstock.com

73 left bird tracks © elsen029 / iStockphoto.com; **right** snow-covered tree © Marina_Poushkina / iStockphoto.com

79 eastern screech owl © stanley45 / iStockphoto.com

INDEX